players

logos

design center

PLAYERS

84 ANTONIO BROWN

28 ADRIAN PETERSON

3

13 ODELL
BECKHAM JR.

29 ERIC BERRY

29 ERIC BERRY

12 TOM BRADY

12 TOM
BRADY

6

DREW
BREES

9

9 DREW
BREES

88 DEZ BRYANT

8

31 KAM CHANCELLOR

21 EZEKIEL ELLIOTT

21 EZEKIEL ELLIOTT

LARRY
FITZGERALD

LARRY
FITZGERALD

11

88 JIMMY GRAHAM

18 A.J. GREEN

87 ROB
GRONKOWSKI

87 ROB
GRONKOWSKI

14

13 T.Y. HILTON

13 T.Y. HILTON

DEANDRE HOPKINS

10

16

31 DAVID JOHNSON

18

JULIO
JONES

JULIO
JONES

19

52 KHALIL MACK

52 KHALIL
MACK

20

15 BRANDON
MARSHALL

15 BRANDON MARSHALL

21

58 VON MILLER

58 VON
MILLER

58

22

CAM
NEWTON

CAM
NEWTON

23

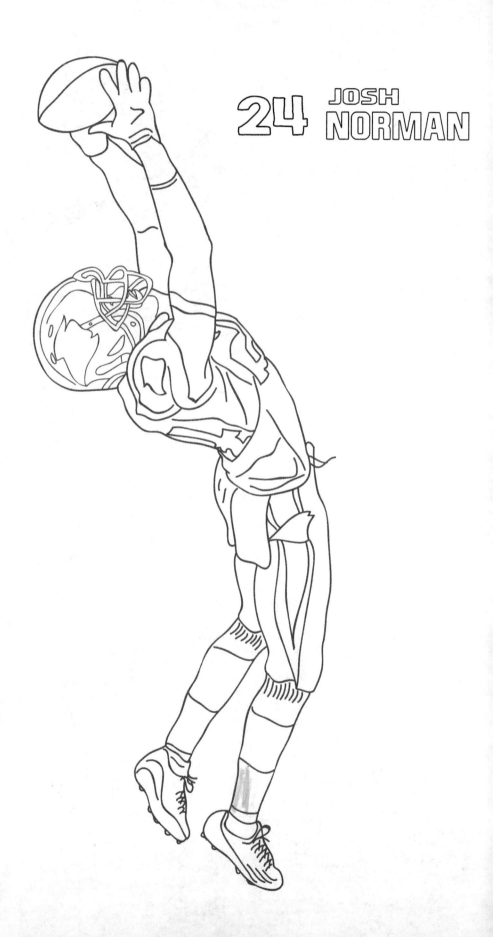

24 JOSH NORMAN

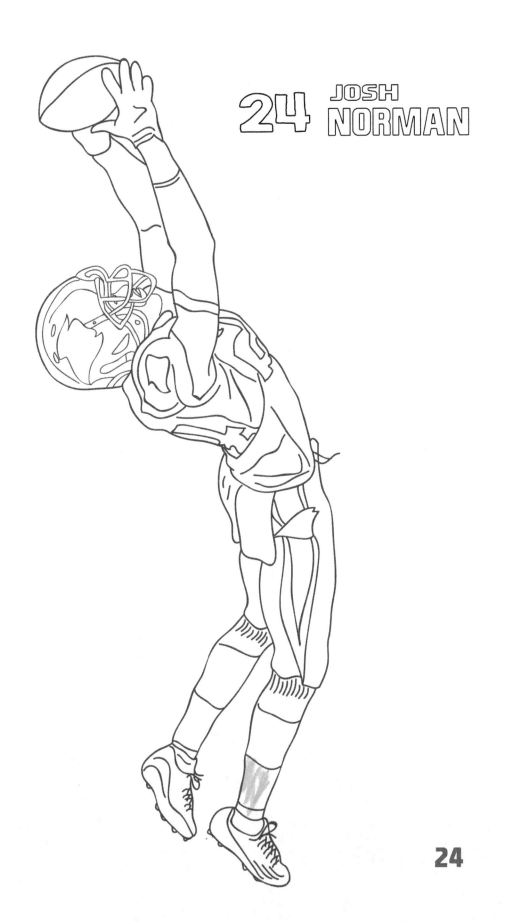

24 JOSH
NORMAN

24

88 GREG
OLSEN

88 GREG OLSEN

25

3 CARSON
PALMER

3 CARSON
PALMER

21 PATRICK PETERSON

27

12 AARON RODGERS

12 AARON RODGERS

28

25 RICHARD
SHERMAN

25 RICHARD
SHERMAN

29

29 EARL THOMAS

99 J.J.
WATT

99 J.J. WATT

3 RUSSELL WILSON

32

LOGOS

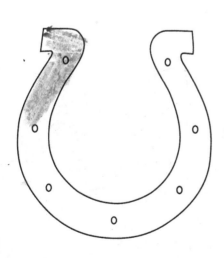

34

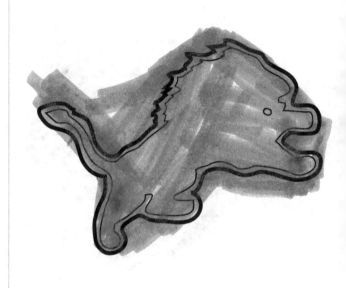

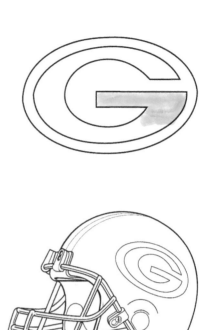

SEAHAWKS
SEATTLE

36

37

DESIGN CENTER

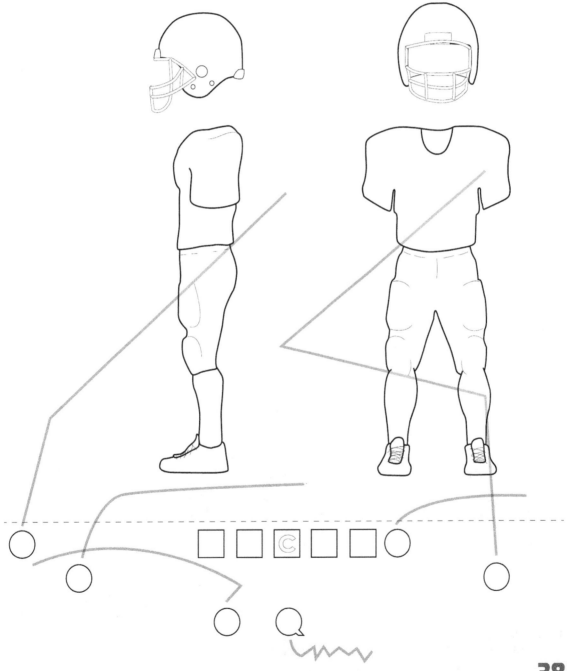

39

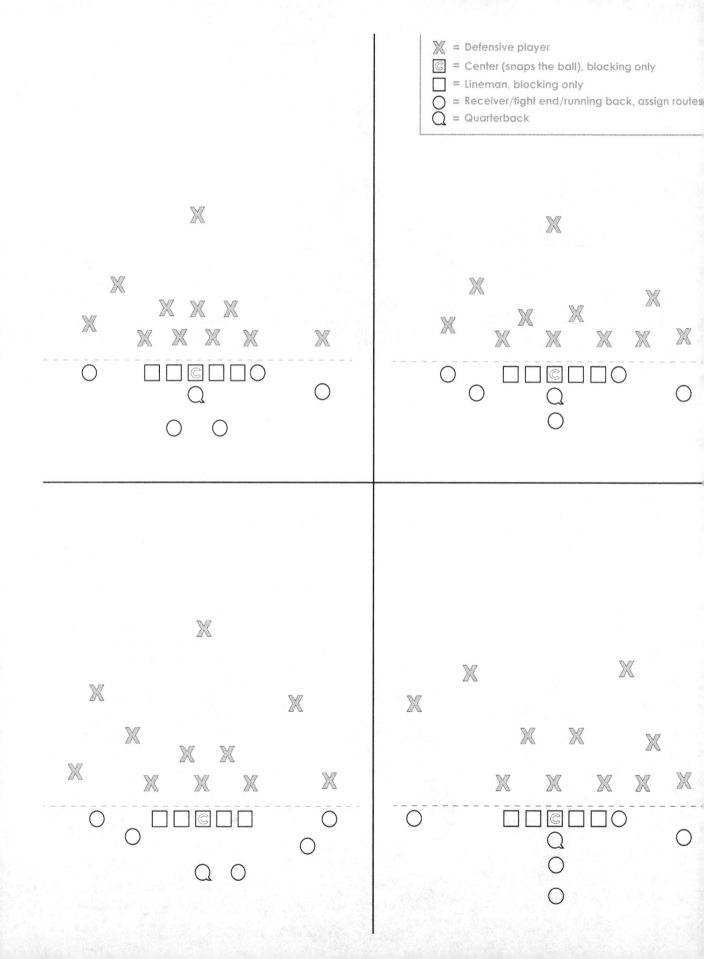

X = Defensive player
C = Center (snaps the ball), blocking only
□ = Lineman, blocking only
○ = Receiver/tight end/running back, assign routes
Q = Quarterback

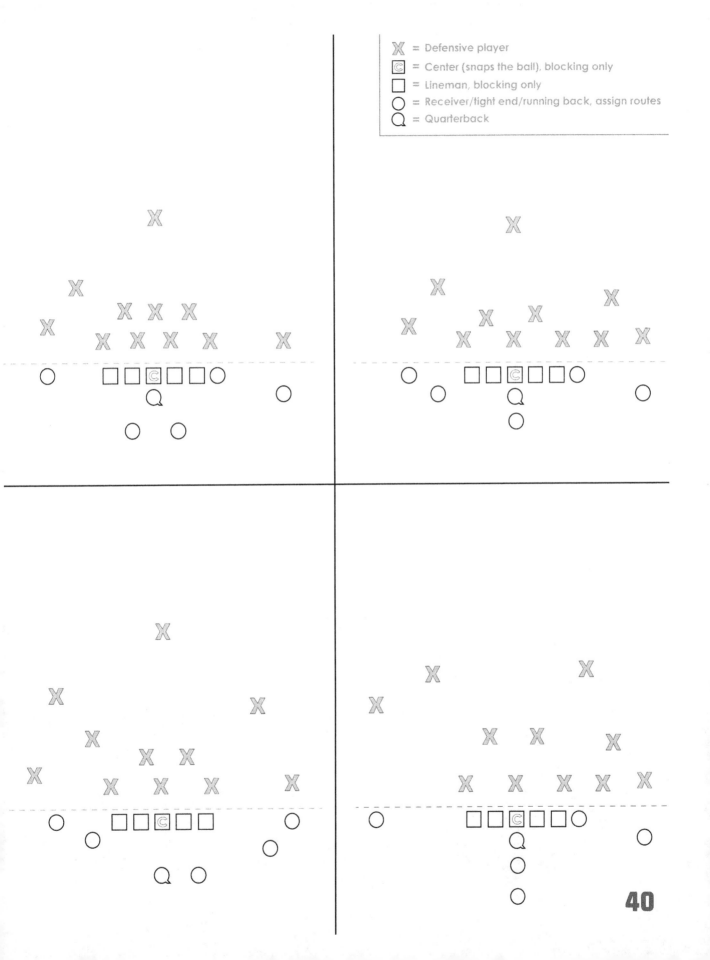

X = Defensive player
C = Center (snaps the ball), blocking only
□ = Lineman, blocking only
O = Receiver/tight end/running back, assign routes
Q = Quarterback

40

DRAW YOUR OWN
(You get 11 *total* players)

☐ ☐ 🔲 ☐ ☐
Q

☐ ☐ 🔲 ☐ ☐
Q

☐ ☐ 🔲 ☐ ☐
Q

☐ ☐ 🔲 ☐ ☐
Q

☐ ☐ 🔲 ☐ ☐
Q

☐ ☐ 🔲 ☐ ☐
Q

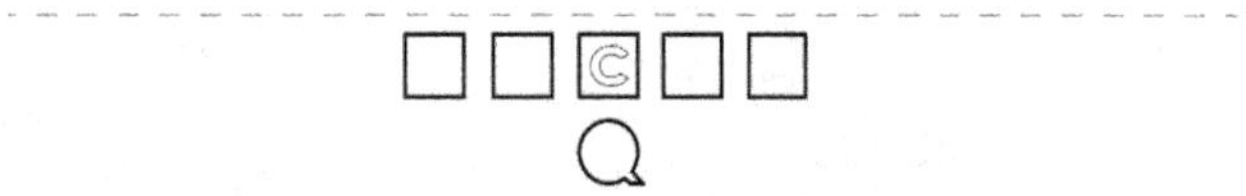

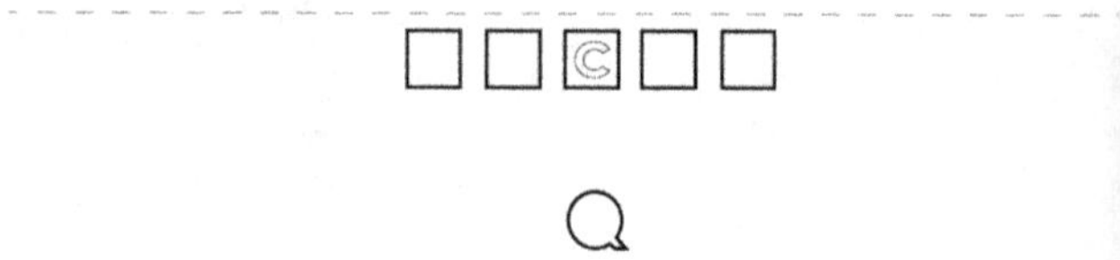

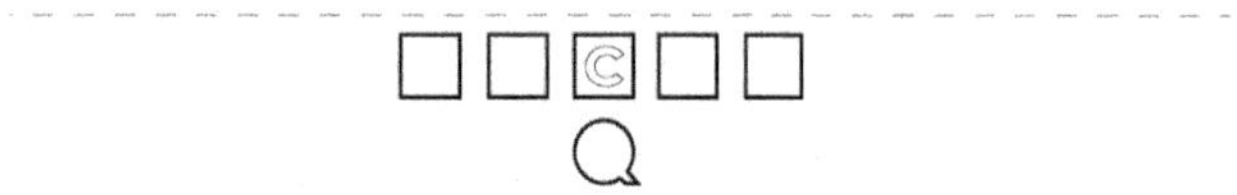

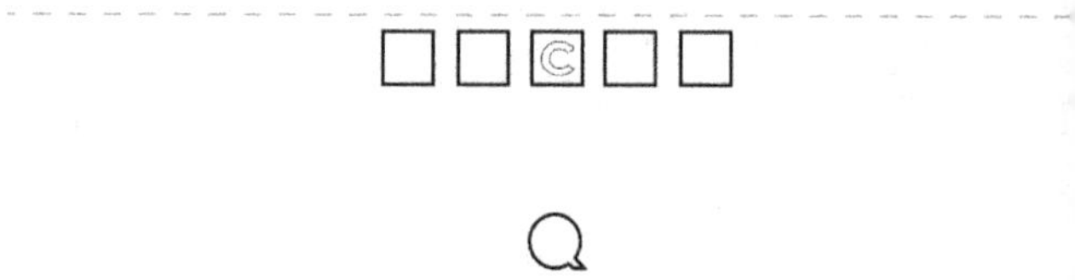

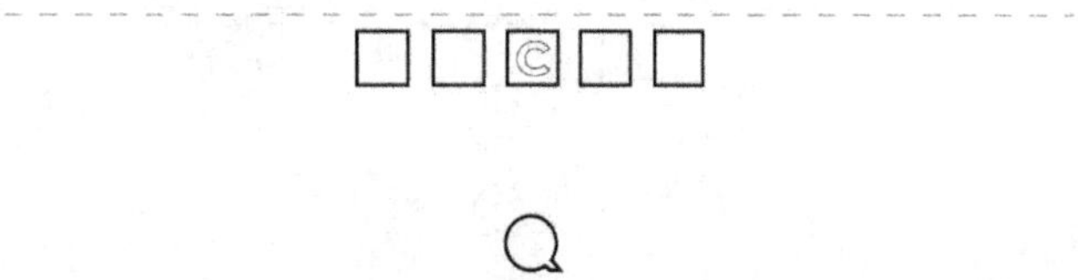

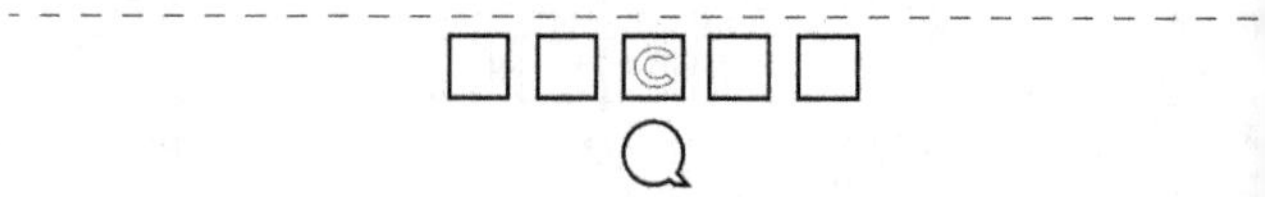

Ⓒ = Center (snaps the ball), blocking only
☐ = Lineman, blocking only
◯ = Receiver/tight end/running back, assign routes
Q = Quarterback

☐☐Ⓒ☐☐
Q

☐☐Ⓒ☐☐
Q

☐☐Ⓒ☐☐
Q

☐☐Ⓒ☐☐
Q

☐☐Ⓒ☐☐
Q

☐☐Ⓒ☐☐
Q

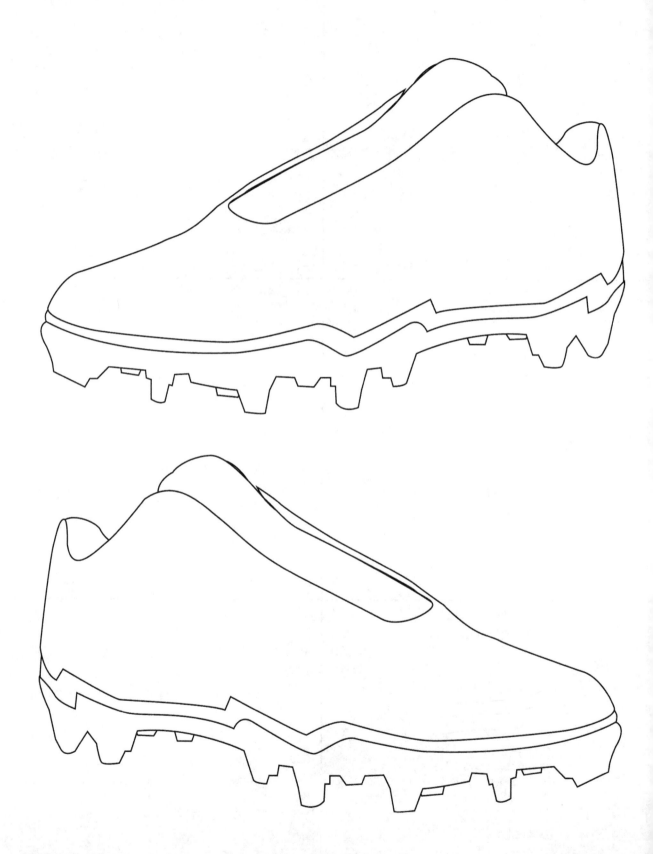

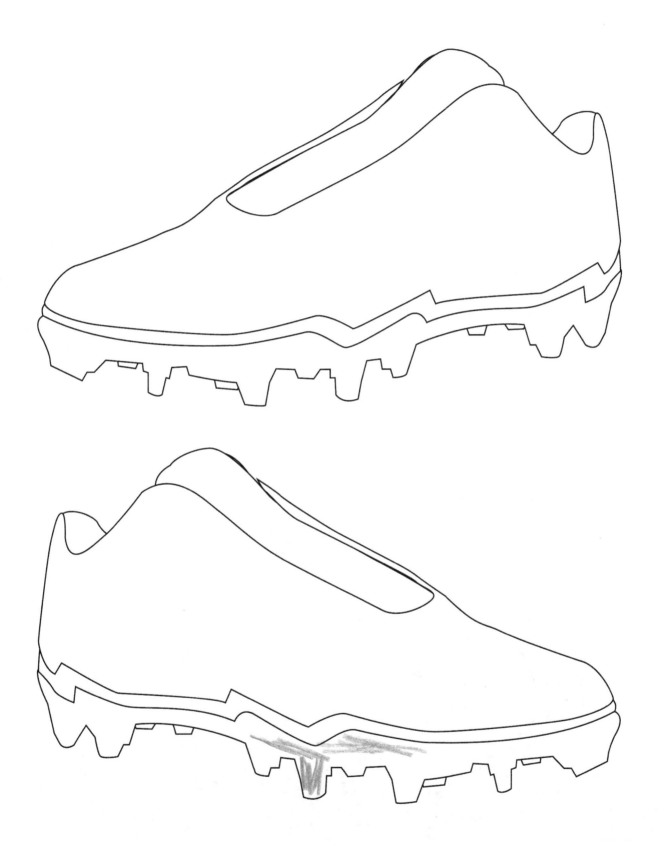

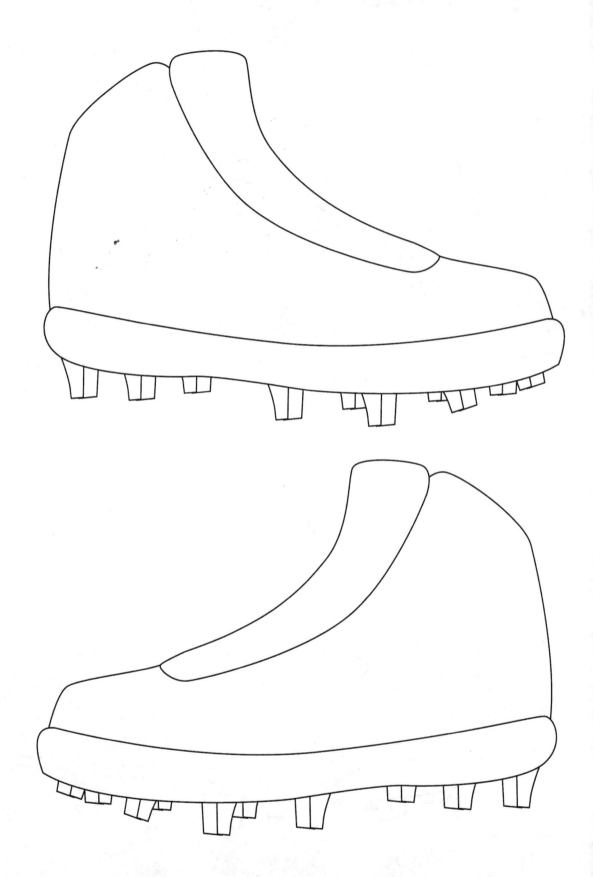

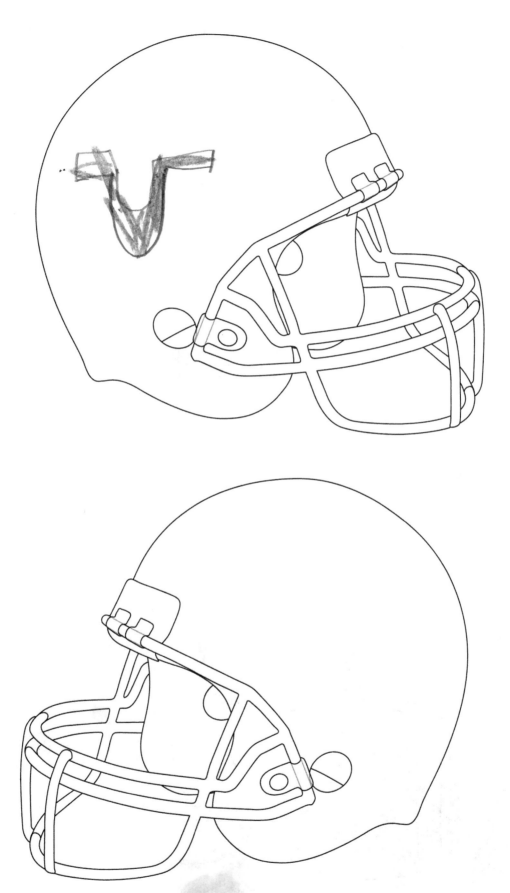

44

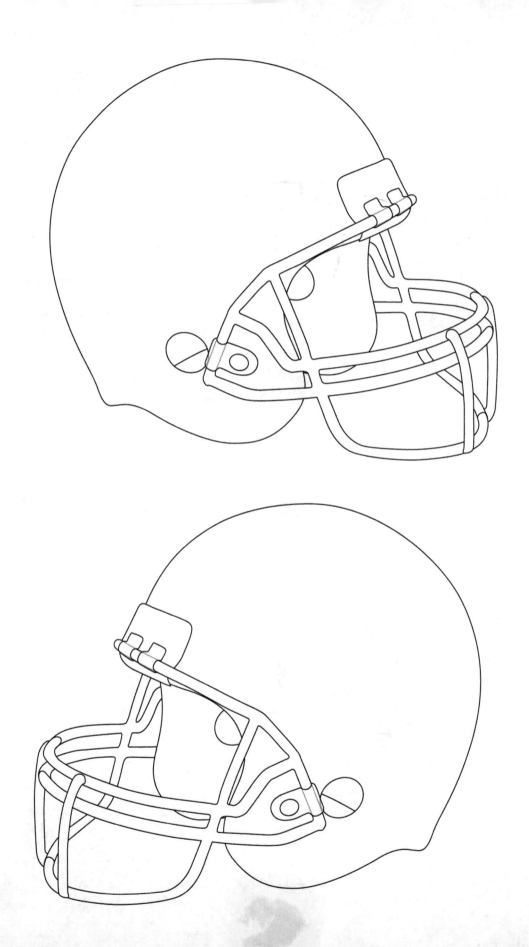

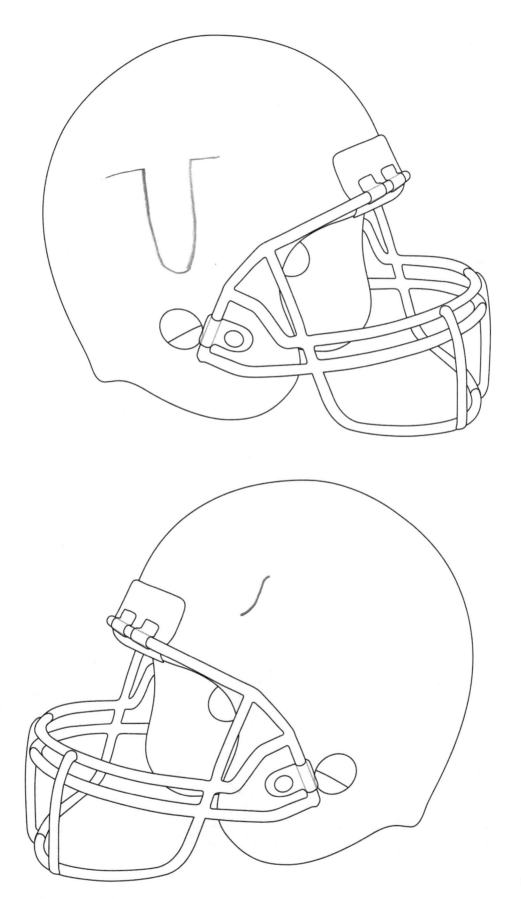

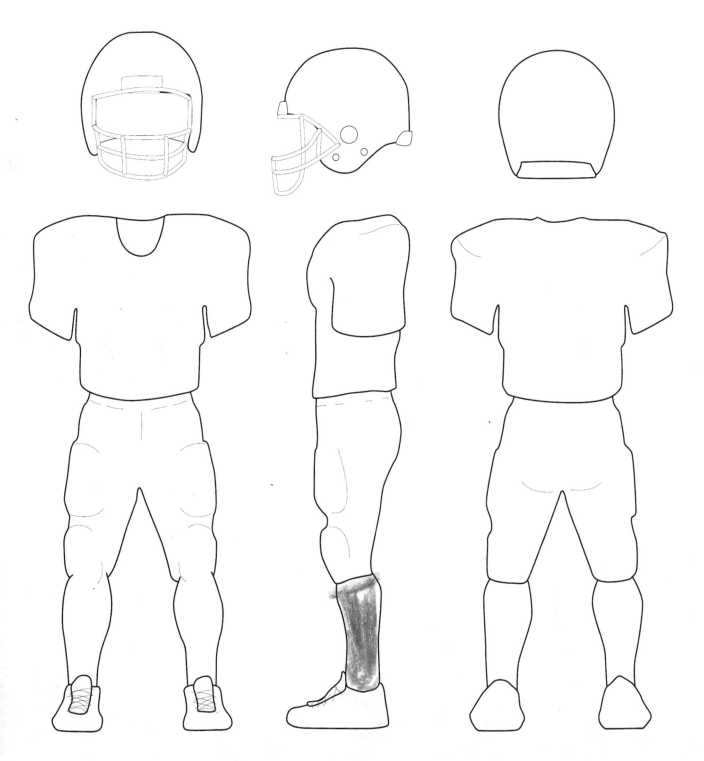

46

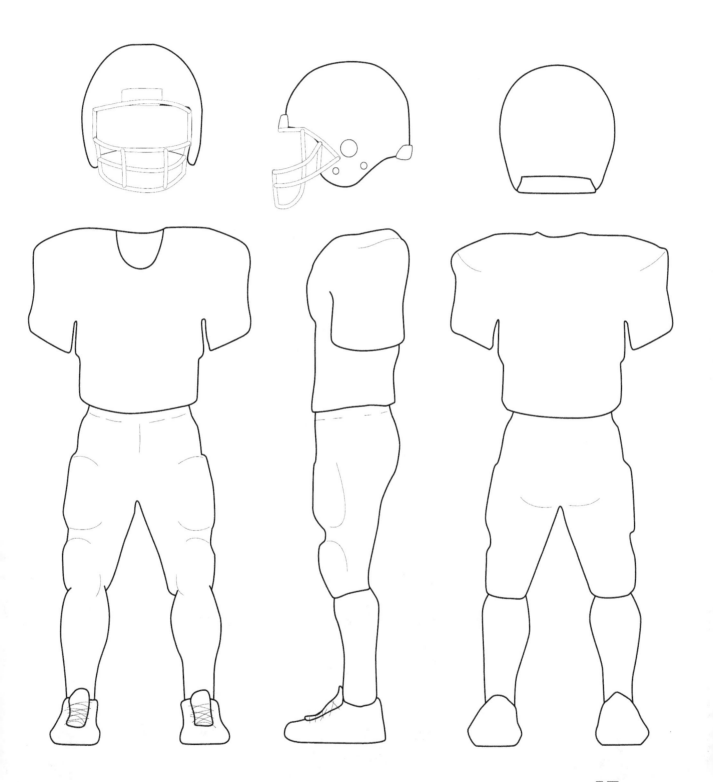